The Senses

SIGHT

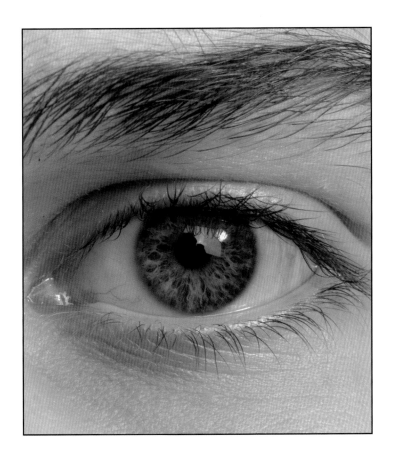

Angela Royston

Chrysalis Children's Books

First published in the UK in 2005 by
Chrysalis Children's Books
An imprint of Chrysalis Books Group Plc,
The Chrysalis Building, Bramley Road,
London W10 6SP

ISBN 1 84458 165 9

British Library Cataloguing in Publication Data
for this book is available from the British Library.

Editorial Manager *Joyce Bentley*
Senior Editor *Rasha Elsaeed*
Editorial Assistant *Camilla Lloyd*

Produced by Bender Richardson White
Project Editor *Lionel Bender*
Designer *Ben White*
Production *Kim Richardson*
Picture Researcher *Cathy Stastny*
Cover Make-up *Mike Pilley, Radius*

Printed in China

10 9 8 7 6 5 4 3 2 1

Words in **bold** can be found in New words on page 31.

Typography *Natascha Frensch*
Read Regular, READ SMALLCAPS and Read Space; European Community Design Registration 2003
and Copyright © Natascha Frensch 2001-2004 Read Medium, **Read Black** and *Read Slanted*
Copyright © Natascha Frensch 2003-2004

READ™ is a revolutionary new typeface that will enchance children's understanding through clear, easily
recognisable character shapes. With its evenly spaced and carefully designed characters, READ™ will help
children at all stages to improve their literacy skills, and is ideal for young readers, reluctant readers and
especially children with dyslexia.

Picture credits
Cover: Bubbles/Jennie Woodcock. **Inside:** Bubbles: pages 4 (Pauline Cutler), 5 (Lucy Tizard), 6 (Lucy Tizard), 8 (Loisjoy
Thurstun), 12 (Frans Rombout), 13 (Jacqui Farrow), 16 (Lucy Tizard), 18 (Jennie Woodcock), 20 (Ian West), 21 (Jennie
Woodcock), 22 (Loisjoy Thurstun), 26 (Jennie Woodcock). Educationphotos.co.uk/Walmsley: pages 15, 23, 25. Steve
Gorton: pages 1, 2, 7, 9, 10, 11, 14, 17, 19, 24, 27, 28, 29.

Contents

What is sight? 4

Kinds of eyes 6

Light to see in 8

How you see 10

Seeing colours 12

Near and far 14

A clear picture 16

Wearing glasses 18

Eye tests 20

Blindness 22

Seeing more 24

Eye care 26

Healthy eyes 28

Quiz 30

New words 31

Index 32

What is sight?

Sight is the **sense** that lets you see things. You use sight to look at people, places and objects.

Your eyes and brain work together
to give you sight.

Kinds of eyes

Different people have different sizes, shapes and colours of eyes.

You close your **eyelids** to shut your eyes. Eyelids and eyelashes protect your eyes.

Light to see in

You cannot see when there is no light. You need a torch or candle to see in the **dark**.

In **dim** light you can see shapes but few colours.

How you see

You see when light gets inside your eyes. A mirror sends light from your face into your eyes.

Light gets into each eye through the black hole in the middle.

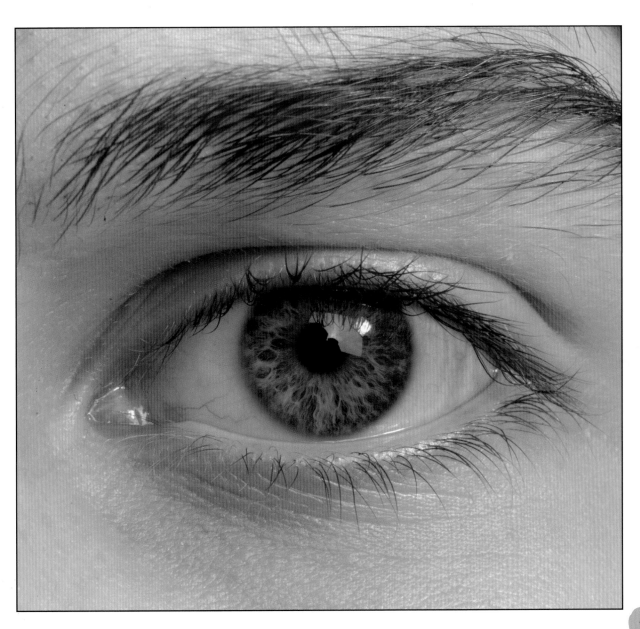

Seeing colours

In bright light you can see lots
of different colours.

Some colours are bright. Other colours are pale. Some colours look dark.

Near and far

Your eyes can see things that are very near and things that are far away.

You can tell something is close because it looks bigger than it does when far away.

A clear picture

The girl on the right is clear because she is **in focus**.

If you **focus** on something close to you, the things behind it look **blurred**.

Wearing glasses

Some people wear glasses, or spectacles, to help them see clearly.

These glasses make the words look bigger and clearer.

Montagu Court
Gosforth,
Newcastle
Upon Tyne

...ide it feels like ...anhattan,' quips the glossy brochure for this ...torey tower.

...Pros Even anti-modernists must admit that this svelte, glass blade is elegant. If you can afford one of the six penthouses, you'll have London prostrate before you, all of ...hich you can survey

a palette of hardwood sliding doors and full-height windows.
Cons Look south, and view is of similar sleek glass beasties, but the hinterland is an unlovely sprawl of expressways and housing estates. ...apartments have th... own outside spa...
Price From £...
for a tw...

...e **Panoramic**
Richmond Hill,
Bournemouth

It's a high building on a high hill so it should live up to its name.
Pros You can see as far as

September so you'll h... to buy off-plan.
Price From £166,00... for a one-bedroom fl... to £399,950 for thre... bedrooms. FPD Savil... 01202 856883.

Eye tests

A doctor or **optician** tests how well you can see large and small letters.

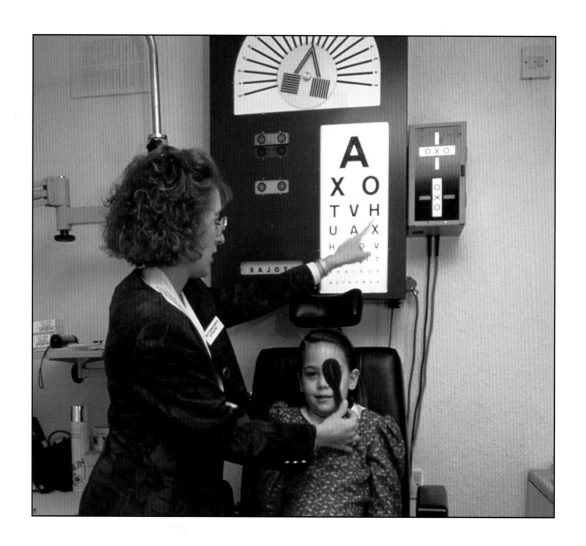

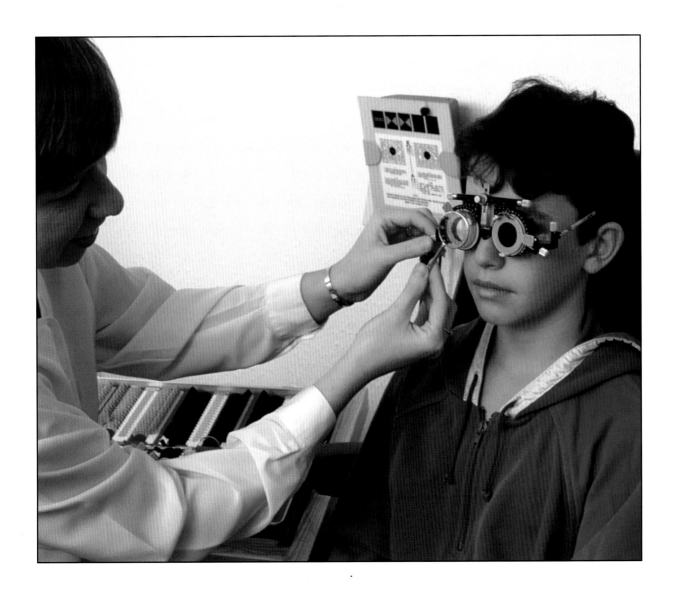

The doctor uses special glasses
to test your sight.

Blindness

Blind people can hardly see anything.
This is like being **blindfolded.**

Blind people find their way around by touching things. They use a long stick to help them.

Seeing more

Binoculars are special glasses that make things look bigger and closer.

A **magnifying glass** makes small things look bigger and clearer.

Eye care

Wear **sunglasses** or a hat to protect your eyes from sunshine. Never look straight at the sun.

If you get an eye **infection**, you will need special cream or bathing liquid to cure it.

Healthy eyes

These foods contain **vitamins** that are good for eyesight.

Wash your eyelids carefully when you wash your face.

Quiz

1 What do eyelids do?

2 What do you need to see with at night?

3 How does light get inside your eye?

4 Why do some people wear glasses?

5 Why do blind people use a stick?

6 What does a magnifying glass do?

7 Why should you wear sunglasses in strong sunlight?

8 Which foods help to keep your eyes healthy?

The answers are all in this book!

New words

binoculars special glasses that make faraway things look bigger and nearer.

blindfold something that covers your eyes and stops you seeing anything.

blurred fuzzy, not clear.

dark when there is hardly any light.

dim when there is not enough light to see well.

eyelashes hairs at the edge of your eyelid.

eyelid flap of skin that opens and closes over your eye.

focus make something look sharp and clear.

infection an illness that you catch from someone else.

in focus when something looks sharp and clear.

magnifying glass curved glass that makes small things look bigger.

optician person who tests eyes and sells glasses.

sense the way you find out about your surroundings. You have five senses – sight, hearing, smell, taste and touch.

sunglasses dark glasses that protect your eyes from sunlight.

vitamins chemicals in food that your body needs to work properly and to stay healthy.

Index

binoculars 24

blindness 22–23

blurred 17

colours 6, 9, 12–13

dark 8, 13

eyelashes 7

eyelids 7, 29

eyes 5, 6–7, 10, 11, 14,
    26–27, 28–29

focus 16, 17

glasses 18–19, 21, 24

infection 27

light 8–9, 10, 11

mirror 10

optician 20

seeing 4, 8, 9, 10, 12,
    14, 18, 22

sense 4, 5

sunglasses 26